# POLITICAL
# MANIPULATION

**PHILIP STEELE**

Heinemann
**LIBRARY**

# www.heinemann.co.uk/library
Visit our website to find out more information about **Heinemann Library** books.

To order:
 Phone 44 (0) 1865 888066
 Send a fax to 44 (0) 1865 314091
Visit the Heinemann bookshop at www.heinemann.co.uk/library to browse our catalogue and order online.

First published in Great Britain by Heinemann Library, Halley Court, Jordan Hill, Oxford OX2 8EJ, part of Harcourt Education.

Heinemann is a registered trademark of Harcourt Education Ltd.

Created, designed and produced for Heinemann Library by Trocadero Publishing, An Electra Media Group Enterprise, Suite 204, 74 Pitt Street, Sydney, Australia

Originated by Modern Age
Printed in China
by WKT

ISBN 0 431 09834 4
10 09 08 07 06
10 9 8 7 6 5 4 3 2 1

**British Library Cataloguing in Publication Data**
Steele, Philip
Influence and Persuasion: Political Manipulation – The World of Spin
306.2
A full catalogue record for this book is available from the British Library.

Picture credits
Brand X Pictures 5, 6, 12 (left), 30, 31, 36, 38, 46, 49, 50, 57, 58, 59; Corbis/Jose Luis Pelaez cover; Corbis/Reuters 45; Electra Collection 13; Ericsson 22; FairfaxPhotos/ Robert Pearce 21; FairfaxPhotos/Pat Scala 24; FairfaxPhotos/Penny Bradfield 35; Flat Earth Picture Gallery 14, 54; Greenpeace/Michel Le Moine 11; Kobal Collection/Columbia Pictures 32; Magnum/Raghu Rai 44; Oronsay Imagery/Scott Brodie 12 (right), 53, 56; Popperfoto 51; US Army 40, 41; US National Archives 16, 17, 19, 20, 21 (top), 48; US Navy 39; US Department of Defense 8, 23, 25, 26 (bottom), 28, 29; US State Department 26 (top)

# contents

# introduction

On Thursday 30 September 2004, two men stood under the television lights in Florida. That American state had recently been battered by hurricanes, but another story led the news broadcasts. The Republican president of the USA, George W. Bush, was taking part in the first televised public debate with his rival in the forthcoming presidential election, Democratic contender John Kerry. The winner in that election would become the most powerful person in the world, whose chosen policies would affect the lives not just of Americans but of countless others. What would be said in Florida that night was of great importance.

However, members of the rival political campaign teams were concentrating less on the content of the debate than on other matters. How high were the lecterns for the candidates' notes? On television, would George W. Bush look too short? Would John Kerry look too tall? What was the temperature in the room? Everyone remembered how Richard M. Nixon had, according to many commentators, lost the presidential election to John F. Kennedy in September 1960 because he looked unwell after a knee injury and did not wear make-up for the television. Under the studio lights Nixon had looked pasty-faced and sweaty. The candidates had very similar levels of support, so the number of people influenced by the television pictures may have been sufficient to change the outcome of the election.

In 2004, nothing would be allowed to put one candidate at a disadvantage. The rules of engagement had been carefully drawn up: no bodily contact, no direct questioning, and no audience reactions would be broadcast. After the debate, both sides claimed victory and attempted to present their own candidate's weaknesses as strengths. The press reported the event more as if it were some wrestling contest than as a debate that would affect war and peace, the global environment, jobs, or taxation.

To many observers, the stage management of the presidential debate made it unnatural, and detracted from the real issues. They felt that it was just one more example of the descent of politics into a battle of "spin", the presentation of information in a way that will create the least possible public hostility, and the greatest possible advantage to the client. A pitcher in baseball, or a bowler in cricket, learns how to spin or swing the ball in order to deceive the batter or batsman. Politicians' aims had become very similar. Some people claimed that spin had become an unhealthy obsession in all maspects of political life.

# A rule book for rulers

Niccoló Machiavelli (1469–1527) was a politician and diplomat in Florence, Italy. When he lost his job in 1512, he decided to write a guide to governing nations. The result was a book called *The Prince*, which he wrote in 1513. It was published in 1515 and is still a best-seller today. Machiavelli had little time for honesty or integrity in politics. He believed that political manipulation was the quickest route to success. If the best interests of the state demanded it, he thought, a ruler should lie, cheat, or fight to get his own way.

Machiavelli wrote: "One sees from the experience of our times that the princes who have accomplished great deeds are those who have cared little for keeping their promises, and who have known how to manipulate the minds of men by shrewdness."

To this day, any manipulative or devious political scheme is said to be "Machiavellian". Some politicians do not accept Machiavelli's ideas. He seems to them to represent all that is worst in their profession. Others think he simply lived in the real world, and believe that in politics a good end may justify rather doubtful means.

Spin has become widespread in recent years. It affects the news we read or hear every day, and has itself become part of the news. Headline after headline tells of spin and of the people who are experts at news management, the so-called "spin doctors" or "spinmeisters".

Spin is just one of a wide range of strategies that politicians use to gain acceptance of their policies and plans. Such tactics could be called "political manipulation", and are worthy of close study. Is political manipulation a new development? What forms does it take? Who manipulates whom, and how? Do their tactics work? Are they right or wrong? Are these tactics legal? How do they affect us?

# Who invented politics?

Politics has existed ever since people first established towns, nations, and empires. It was simply the way in which these cities and states could be organized and made to work.

The word *politics* comes from the word *polis*, which meant "city" in the ancient Greek language. About 2500 years ago, most Greek states were small, based around individual cities. Their inhabitants were schemers and dreamers, philosophers who loved to talk about society, politics, and power.

The Greeks tried out many different types of government. They invented democracy, which is "government by the people". Using the term "democracy" might itself be considered an early example of spin because, for all their talk of "the people", the Greeks allowed no vote to women, slaves, or foreign-born citizens. "The people" meant only freeborn males who had been born and raised in the city.

## Are we being fooled?

Political decisions concern every aspect of our lives. They determine how we work, how we play, how we treat each other, how we trade and spend our money, what we learn, what we can do, and what we cannot. We therefore need to know how political policies are presented to us. Are we being told the truth? Are we being misled? Perhaps the most important question of all is: How do we recognize political manipulation when it happens?

*The spinning child's top is intended to bedazzle and intrigue. The art of "spin", as practiced in politics, is intended to have the same effect on the public.*

# what is political manipulation?

First, we need to define what we are talking about. What do we mean by the words "politics" and "manipulation"?

Politics is the art of getting things done, of putting forward ideas or programmes for social or economic change. It may also be about trying to prevent change. Politics concerns itself with the way in which people are represented or ruled, with government, and with making new laws. It deals with nations and how they relate to each other, with treaties, with war and peace, with international alliances, and with trading organizations.

*US Secretary of Defense Donald Rumsfeld (right) with USAF General Richard Myers at a Pentagon press conference. Such conferences are often used by politicians to influence the media, and through them the population in general.*

People who study politics also look at the bigger picture. They consider how people have lived, worked, and organized themselves throughout history. They try to find out why events occurred as and when they did. They see if current political problems are rooted in the past, and consider how we can learn from these lessons and move forward.

The literal meaning of "manipulation" is "movement of something by hand". From this it has come to have implications of alteration, management, interference, or presenting facts in a particular way. The word has taken on more negative meanings, too. "Manipulation" may suggest artfulness, deviousness, fiddling things, or taking advantage of someone.

## Methods of manipulation

The phrase "political manipulation" therefore refers to any strategy that is designed to change or influence a political outcome. It may involve no more than the straightforward communication of information: if one gives people the facts, they may be persuaded of the case one is making. On the other hand, persuasion may include more complicated tactics such as "spin", in which clever presentation may disguise the true nature of the information being communicated.

Political manipulation may also involve outright deception, threats, bribery, or violence: methods that many people think are immoral. By contrast, politicians who do not use such "low" tactics may persuade people of their case because of their honesty and integrity. This tactic is sometimes called "seizing the moral high ground", because they make themselves appear morally superior to their opponents.

## Relatives of spin

Political manipulation involves tactics used in many other areas of life, including social control, and commerce. These tactics include censorship (controlling information, or limiting free expression); propaganda (spreading information, which is often misleading or false, in order to gain support for a particular cause); advertising (promoting products or services to consumers); and public relations (PR; encouraging a favourable response to a person, company, or government policy).

# who pulls the strings?

The world of politics can seem like a puppet show. The journalist writes, the television pundit talks, and the politician makes fine speeches, but it is very hard for the public to tell who is pulling the strings. Any of these people may be using tactics of political manipulation.

## Political professionals

The chief political manipulators are politicians, whether national, regional, or local. In a democracy, their aims are to convince the public so that they win its support, and to discredit the opposition. They do this partly because they believe their policies are the best ones for the community. They do it also because they need to persuade the public in order to get enough votes to win the next election. If they do not win the election, they may lose their jobs.

"The rulers of the state are the only ones who should have the privilege of lying, either at home or abroad; they may be allowed to lie for the good of the state."

Plato, Greek philosopher, approx. 428–348 BC

It is not only against each other that political parties wage wars of spin. There are always rival individuals or factions within a party who wish to promote their own policies, so manipulation takes place within parties as well as between them. Even when there is a democratic structure for agreeing things, such as a policy-making conference, there is scope for wheeling, dealing, and fixing.

On the international stage, governments may use diplomacy, threats, sanctions, or even warfare to achieve their national aims. Much negotiation – and manipulation – takes place within the framework of international treaties, alliances, and organizations.

## The campaigners

Other political players include non-governmental organizations (NGOs), which campaign or take action over issues such as the environment, healthcare, famine, or human rights. They may have strong political objectives, and need to influence international organizations, governments, political parties, commercial companies, and the general public to achieve the changes they want. The big NGOs, such as Amnesty International, Greenpeace, and the Worldwide Fund for Nature (WWFN), are very skilled operators and have earned themselves public respect, especially in Europe.

*Greenpeace activists climb the rock face above France's Mirabeau Tunnel to protest the transport of plutonium by road convoy.*

Charities, pressure groups, and members of the public who protest about any number of issues, from animal rights to nuclear weapons to abortion, need to learn the tactics of political campaigning, even if on only a local level, to be successful.

## With God on their side

It would be wrong to think that religious groups such as mosques, churches, and temples, are above politics. Rabbis, imams, priests, and monks may call upon the services of spin doctors.

They may campaign for or against government policies on issues such as education, marriage, dress, poverty, healthcare, family planning, and sex education.

Religion is deeply woven into the fabric of many long-standing political disputes and armed conflicts around the world, including those between Catholic and Protestant Christians in Northern Ireland, and between Hindus and Muslims in Kashmir. Even the more peaceful and spiritual religious believers must seek political outcomes in accordance with their faith if they are to engage with the realities of modern life.

## Employers and employees

Businesses and corporations also operate within a political world. They may, for example, object to labour laws that incur high costs for them, or campaign against high rates of taxation. Petroleum companies may oppose environmental laws that limit prospecting for oil, or that try to discourage the use of cars. Tobacco or food companies may object to public health laws. In many parts of the world, politicians have close relationships with large businesses, accepting donations and bribes.

*Religions of all kinds around the world are deeply involved the process of political manipulation, to promote their philosophies and influence governments.*

Trade unions also operate within the political arena: in working to improve the wages or working conditions of their members, they may run up against government policy as well as against company rules. They have to adopt a wide range of political strategies in order to represent their members successfully.

## Media spinners

Radio, television, films, newspapers, magazines, the Internet, and books are together known as "the communications media". They carry or report on the spin that is used by politicians, companies, and lobby groups to convey their messages. However, the media are also major political manipulators themselves. Media owners have their own political beliefs and ambitions, and their own commercial alliances. These may influence how much space or time a publication or programme gives to somebody's opinions. A story may be reported from only one point of view, so that the reader or viewer will draw a particular conclusion. In a newspaper, for instance, the comment pages will make it clear that what is presented is an opinion, but it may be harder to tell whether the news pages are also promoting someone's beliefs. Trying to see past this presentation is called "reading between the lines".

## The power of the press

In the Middle Ages, the barons (senior lords) in what is now the UK were often more powerful than the king himself. One English lord, Richard Neville, Earl of Warwick (1428–1471), became known as "the king-maker", because he could make or break the power of a monarch. Today, leading executives of communications corporations are often called "media barons". Their power is awesome. Media corporations have the money, organization, and influence to out-spin and out-manoeuvre governments, other companies, and the rest of the press – and the public, too.

Rupert Murdoch (born in Adelaide, Australia, in 1931) has built up a media empire in newspapers, book publishing, television, and film across Australia, the UK, the USA, and Asia. Forty per cent of US television viewers watch Murdoch-owned stations. No UK prime minister takes office without first conferring with Rupert Murdoch, because he owns popular tabloid newspapers such as the *Sun* and the *News of the World*, as well as the UK's serious broadsheets *The Times* and *The Sunday Times*. This makes him very influential, because these newspapers often choose to support one particular political party, and this support can affect the votes of many people.

Silvio Berlusconi (born in Milan, Italy, in 1936) owns much of the Italian media. He is a leader of the far-right Forza Italia political party, and has gone one step further than most media barons by becoming Italy's prime minister. Machiavelli would surely be proud of him. Berlusconi's critics say that his newspapers and television stations promote his political interests, and that he passes laws to protect their commercial interests.

*A peaceful scene in Beijing's Tiananmen Square, where one example of people power failed. The democracy movement that flowered briefly here in 1989 was violently crushed by the government.*

## People power

A group of people working together has more power than an individual has. Political parties, big businesses, and media corporations all have political muscle. But can somebody working alone be a political manipulator in his or her own right?

A celebrity may find it easy, if he or she is able to attract attention from the media. The Irish pop star Bob Geldof has led major international campaigns for famine and AIDS relief in Africa since 1984, and has skilfully lobbied politicians and governments. Any individual who is determined can make a mark, especially if he or she learns the mechanics of communication and political campaigning.

It is hard without sufficient funding, however. Political manipulation is much easier for the rich and powerful. Those who have no access to power need to build up a popular movement or political party to achieve their aims. Those who live under repression, with little economic power – the unemployed, for example, refugees, or people who live in states that are not democratic – often resort to direct action, which may be anti-social, illegal, or violent. Governments and large corporations may do the same, but they can employ armies and PR companies to do their work for them.

## Who is the target?

The manipulators' targets may be other governments, members of political parties, journalists and broadcasters, employers, or workers. In a democracy, all of these people have a vote. This makes them all interesting to the manipulators, who want to influence the way people vote.

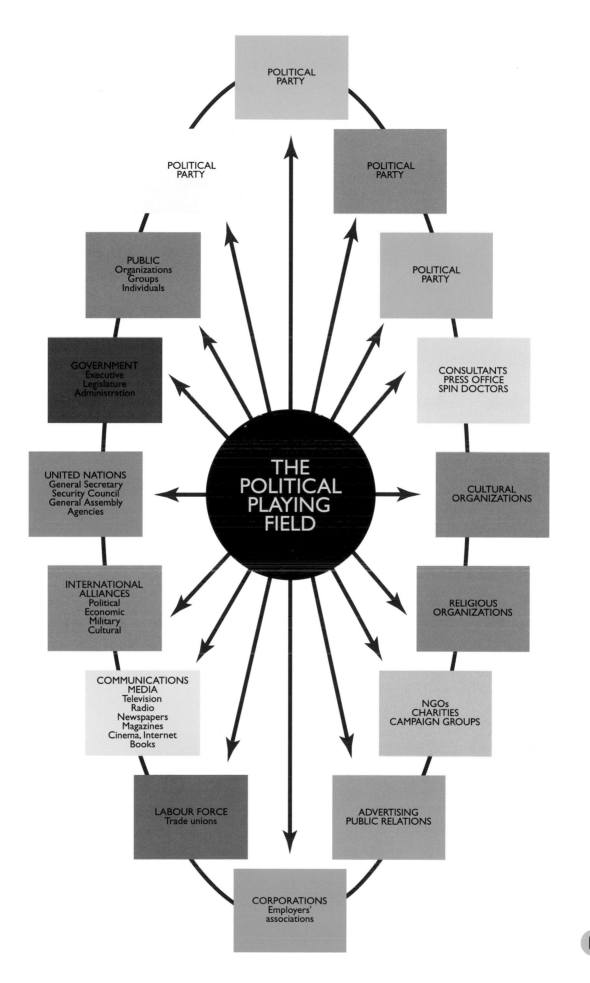

# meet the spin doctors

Political manipulation is nothing new. It was being discussed 2500 years ago in ancient Greece, and roughly 500 years ago in Renaissance Italy. However, spin is a much more modern development, and relies on the existence of mass media for rapid communication with large numbers of people.

## The first spinners

The first printed newspapers began to appear in northern Europe in the 1600s. By the 1800s, they were playing an important role in politics. Napoleon I, the former revolutionary who had himself crowned Emperor of France in 1804, was a master at using the press and manipulating public opinion, as was his nephew, Napoleon III.

*Dwight D. Eisenhower campaigning in 1952. "I Like Ike" was the memorable slogan used to promote the presidential candidate.*

# One big player – The spin firm

One of the worst environmental disasters in modern times was the spill of 11 million gallons of crude oil into Alaskan waters by the *Exxon Valdez* supertanker in 1989. This had huge political, commercial, and environmental impacts. Some 1690 km of Alaskan coastline were covered in oil. Over 5800 seabirds died.

In the five years that followed, the Exxon company had to pay a fine of US$100 million, US$2 billion on cleaning up the mess, US$900 million on civil law suits, and US$5 billion on compensating fishermen for their loss of livelihood. The Exxon company hired Burson-Marsteller, one of the world's biggest public relations companies, to counter press critics and repair its image. This process is called "damage limitation".

Burson-Marsteller has for many years been one of the world's major professional political manipulators. It has represented controversial governments in Argentina, Chile, Nigeria, South Korea, Indonesia, and Romania. It has represented corporations under fire, such as Union Carbide (the owners of a chemical plant in Bhopal in India which accidentally killed thousands of people in 1984) and Louisiana-Pacific Logging (a company which angered conservationists in 1990 by cutting down ancient redwood forest).

Burson-Marsteller has fought against public campaigns and regularly spun in the media against human rights activists, NGOs, and environmentalists.

*Television took a key role in political campaigns in the 1950s, particularly with the 1952 and 1956 presidential campaigns.*

## New media

New forms of mass media were invented in the 20th century: radio, film, and television. Their potential for shaping public opinion was immense. They were seized upon not just by democratic governments but also by the new dictatorships. Adolf Hitler (1889–1945), leader of Nazi Germany and a racist mass-murderer, was transformed by party propaganda into a hero and a dog-lover. Hitler's chief adviser in such matters was Joseph Goebbels, who headed the so-called Ministry of Propaganda and Public Enlightenment. This last phrase is a remarkable example of spin.

## Emperor of the press

Napoleon III (1808–1873), who ruled for a time as an elected French president, and then as French emperor, set up a press office that would be recognizable to any modern spin doctor.

His staff read all opposition papers in minute detail, to see what they were saying. It made sure its "own" journalists were given jobs on newspapers, to get favourable stories published. It paid for new printing presses. It subsidized newspapers that the general public assumed were independent of party loyalties.

It sent out barrages of statistics and propaganda to editors all over France, using the recently invented electric telegraph for immediate effect. It even paid fees for sympathetic articles to be placed in the UK and German press.

Josef Stalin (1879–1953), the brutal leader of Soviet Russia, was presented by his state-controlled media as everybody's favourite uncle. While he privately had the original idealists of the Russian revolution murdered and imprisoned, he puffed genially on his pipe for the cameras. The manipulation was outrageous, but people fell for it, and these men gained the total political power that they craved.

## Ad men and shrinks

In the USA, profiling personality above politics on radio, film, and television was already apparent in the 1950s: it was easier and safer to communicate a personality than a controversial policy. The statement, "Trust me – I'm a normal guy, a family man just like you," might win more support at the polls than a complex economic or foreign policy.

In the 1952 presidential election campaign, professional publicists were brought in to support the Republican candidate, Dwight D. Eisenhower. They had experience in advertising and merchandising. Political parties began to be seen for the first time as brand names, and politicians started to pay as much attention to their images as to their policies. Soon Democratic politicians were queuing up to be given the same treatment.

Principal US spin doctors of the 1950s included James Hagerty,

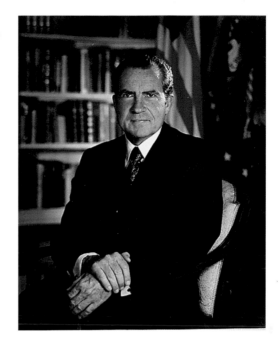

*Richard M. Nixon was accused of corruption when running for Vice President in 1952. He appeared on TV with the family dog, Checkers, which had been given to the Nixons as a gift. Known as the "Checkers Speech", it was considered to have reversed the public's opinion of him.*

press secretary to Eisenhower, and people brought in from outside the official party organization – political press agents such as Clem Whitaker and Leone Baxter (who had joined forces in the 1940s in a successful campaign funded by large pharmaceutical companies against a national health insurance scheme). Another influential spin doctor was Murray Chotiner, who specialized in smearing opponents and hinting that they were communists.

Since 1945, the USA had been vying for power with the communist Soviet Union. Intelligence about the opposition is invaluable to any politician. Membership details, sources of finance, policy discussions, secret files, and campaign plans all provide valuable ammunition in the wrong hands.

In the early 1950s, some US politicians such as Joseph McCarthy had been whipping up a frenzy of anti-communism within the USA, suggesting that all sorts of innocent people were really enemy agents. These were favourite tactics of Richard M. Nixon (1913–1994), who finally won the presidency in 1968 before his political manipulations,

such as breaking into his opponents' offices, were exposed as criminal. He was forced to retire in 1974.

There was another new entrant into the world of US political manipulation in the 20th century: psychology. This is the science of the human mind and the way it works, human nature, and behaviour. The work of the Austrian Sigmund Freud (1856–1939) and the Russian Ivan Pavlov (1849–1936) had inspired a new generation, who now applied psychology to many areas of life, including advertising, marketing, management, work, public relations, and politics. They tried to play on people's personal insecurities, anxieties, guilt, or group instincts to persuade them to buy a certain product or vote a certain way.

# Grandaddy of spin

Edward L. Bernays (1891–1995) was a leading pioneer of public relations in the USA. He was born in Austria, and was a nephew of Sigmund Freud (who studied human behaviour). Bernays aimed to use his uncle's insights into the workings of the human mind to make money in the world of big business. In his career as a PR man, Bernays represented hundreds of leading food companies, manufacturing industries, insurance companies, hotels, publishers, and cultural organizations. On behalf of the tobacco companies, for example, he persuaded countless women to smoke cigarettes.

Bernays' big idea was that, instead of changing products to fit public taste, he would change public tastes to fit the product. He worked behind the scenes, persuading film stars or celebrities to use certain products. In this way he aimed to create demand, to shape a fashion, "a climate of opinion".

Bernays had political as well as commercial clients. In 1924 he set up a campaign for the election of Calvin Coolidge to the presidency. Bernays' master stroke was to bring in stars from show business to support the candidate, so making this rather stern character seem fun-loving and fashionable. This tactic has since become a standard procedure for would-be presidents and prime ministers around the world.

Calvin Coolidge, whose presidential campaign benefited greatly from the skills of Edward L. Bernays.

The manipulation of public opinion in both commerce and politics was now subtle, almost invisible. A best-selling book by an American journalist, Vance Packard, published in 1957, referred to these forces as *The Hidden Persuaders*. Packard (1914–1996) saw this psychological manipulation as a sinister invasion of our minds, an attack on our privacy and free will.

## The age of sound bites

The period of international politics that lasted from 1945 to 1991 was known as the "Cold War". It was a long period of international tension, in which the communist Soviet Union and the capitalist USA competed to be the world's leading power. Both sides employed manipulative techniques, including propaganda, in their efforts to gain the advantage. At the heart of the conflict was ideology: the set of theories and beliefs that make up a political movement. Communism battled with capitalism.

The complexities of the political argument were often reduced to sound bites: small, superficial phrases which can be easily picked up by the press. The headlines often had more effect than the articles that followed them in shaping public opinion.

In March 1983, US President Ronald Reagan delivered an address, drafted by his chief speech-writer Anthony R. Dolan, describing the Soviet Union as "an evil empire".

Republican Reagan was a former film star, and this phrase sounded as if it had come from the movie *Star Wars*. It was a simplistic, subjective phrase, which had been deleted by Reagan's advisers from the drafts of previous speeches. However, the term "evil empire" was immediately picked up by the media, and it stuck very effectively in the minds of the public.

Reagan's chief Cold War ally at this time was the UK Conservative prime minister Margaret Thatcher, dubbed "the Iron Lady" by the Russian press. She was a fierce opponent of communism and socialism, at home and abroad. During a 1984 strike, the UK coal miners of the National Union

*President Ronald Reagan, a fierce opponent of the communist Soviet Union.*

of Miners (NUM) were represented to the press by Thatcher with the sound bite "the enemy within" and were demonized in the popular media. Thatcher's spin won that battle.

*Prime Minister Margaret Thatcher, dubbed the "Iron Lady" by the Russian press.*

## Spin's golden age

The Cold War ended in 1991, with the collapse of the Soviet Union. The battle between communism and capitalism no longer dominated the news. A new generation of leaders was taking charge and, to them, politics was more about management techniques than about ideology. They seemed to some people to be obsessed with what was now generally being called "spin", a term first used by American journalists in the late 1970s.

In the USA, a Democrat called Bill Clinton won the 1992 battle for the presidency. A firm of political consultants, Carville and Begala, set up an efficient campaign headquarters, and played a key role in Clinton's victory. Chief spin doctor James Carville was a master of the new campaigning style, based on a rapid response to events, and damage limitation. He joined President Clinton's team as the senior political adviser. Clinton's team no longer saw their job as a finite campaign leading to the next election. It was ongoing, tireless, and never-ending. It was "the permanent campaign". Carville's headquarters were in "the war room", a phrase used as the title for a 1993 documentary movie about the campaign.

The UK's Labour Party, out of office since 1979, took heart at the Democrats' success in the USA, and seized upon their new techniques of political manipulation. Labour regained power in 1997, under the leadership of Tony Blair. Blair and fellow Labour politicians such as Peter Mandelson dropped the party's long-standing commitment to socialist policies, and rebranded the Labour Party as "New Labour".

"Give me the writing of a nation's advertising and propaganda, and I care not who governs in politics."

Hugh MacLennan, Canadian writer, in 1960

## e-Politicians

Personal computers for the home and office were invented in 1975, mobile phones in 1984, and the Internet computer network in 1987. By the 1990s these tools were being used for campaigning and high-speed management of political crises. There was no longer any need to rummage through dusty files in search of a speech once made by one's opponent. It could be accessed in a second. Pagers allowed speech-makers to be kept constantly "on message", because it became possible to contact people even when they were not in their offices. This meant that as soon as something happened, all relevant people could be informed of it and of the party line, so they could present a united front.

Bill Clinton meets a US Navy sailor at the Pentagon in Washington DC. Clinton relied heavily on spin doctor James Carville during his 1992 campaign for the presidency.

Proposed reforms were always presented as "modernization", thereby suggesting that any opposition came from old-fashioned "stick-in-the-muds", and was not worth listening to

The term "modernization" was picked up unquestioningly by many members of the media. Describing a product as "new" is an old advertising trick, but it seemed to work for Blair in his first term of office, just as it had worked for advertisers of soap powder in the 1960s.

Born in 1957, Alastair Campbell was a journalist who became Tony Blair's spokesman in 1994. After Labour's victory in the general election of 1997, he became press secretary to the new government, presiding over one of the most frantic and determined programmes of political spin ever devised. He was an expert at news management, forever

intervening personally, placing stories, and vociferously attacking critics. He became the first non-elected politician in Britain to be allowed to direct civil servants. (British civil servants are supposed to be free of political affiliation. Unlike in the USA, it is unusual for non-elected UK officials to have power and influence.)

After 2001, now director of communications, Campbell became embroiled in a series of political controversies over the forthcoming war in Iraq. A dossier published by the government in February 2003, making the case for war, was found to contain outdated information taken without permission from a thesis published on the Internet. It became known as "the dodgy dossier".

In the summer of 2003, after the war had begun, a BBC journalist reported that a source in British intelligence was accusing Campbell of having also embellished and exaggerated intelligence in an earlier dossier, in order to spin the case for war. Campbell was enraged and demanded apologies from the BBC. The source was under such pressure that he committed suicide. An inquiry cleared Campbell of responsibility, but blamed careless reporting by the BBC. The journalist was sacked, and the director-general and chairman of the BBC were forced from their posts by the governors.

*Prime Minister Tony Blair, whose government makes extensive use of highly experienced spin doctors.*

## e-Campaigning

The intensive use of email lists in electoral campaigns is a tactic available to smaller or independent campaigners, as well as to major political parties.

In the USA in 1998, a wrestler called Jesse Ventura (really named James George Janos) stood for election for Governor of Minnesota as a Reform Party candidate. Despite being a complete outsider, he won the election (and later joined the Independence Party), and served until 2002. His victory was widely believed to have been the result of an intensive email-based campaign in which his publicity, organization, contacts, and information were all Internet-based.

However, many people felt that the report was "a whitewash", and many sympathized with the BBC. Campbell had broken one of the golden rules of spin. Instead of managing the news, he had become the news. He resigned from his post.

## Bush's spin maestro

One of the most powerful men in US politics today is Karl Rove, political adviser and leader of the Republicans' US$150 million campaign to re-elect George W. Bush as president in 2004. Few policies or actions are planned by the Republicans without Rove's approval. He was born in Denver, Colorado, in 1950, and was an ardent Republican and supporter of Richard Nixon by the age of nine. He made a name for himself as a ruthless wheeler and dealer in student politics. Kept from military service in the Vietnam War by a college deferment, Rove became known for tricks designed to embarrass his opponents.

In 1973, the year of the Watergate scandal (which ended Nixon's presidency), Rove toured the USA, briefing young Republicans on his controversial methods of campaigning. He was hired by George Bush Sr and befriended Bush's son, the young George W. Bush. He also set up a direct mail company to target likely Republican supporters. In campaigns, Rove is a master of scare tactics, smear, and media diversion, and is a canny political survivor.

The modern age of spin began in the USA, and the tactic wasadopted in the UK during the 1990s. By the start of the new millennium, press reports were talking of spin in Germany, Italy, and Australia, and many other countries. Most of these were developed countries with mass communications media, but by 2004 it was being reported that even Afghan warlords, better known for bullets than ballots, were adopting spin techniques in the presidential election campaign.

## Campaigning by phone

In June 2004, Italian Prime Minister Silvio Berlusconi sent out a text message to every mobile phone in Italy (approximately 30 million phones) telling people to vote in the forthcoming European Union's parliamentary election. He said that this was done as part of a public information service.

His opponents cried foul. They said that all spam (unsolicited messages) was an intrusion into people's privacy, and that the message could be interpreted as a call for support from the governing party. They responded with an anti-Berlusconi text-messaging campaign.

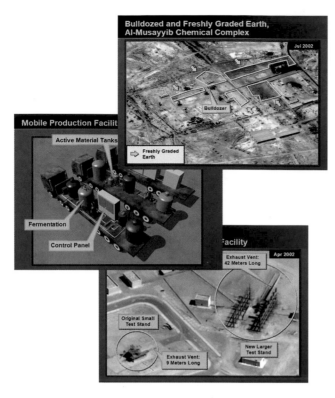

The February 2003 appearance before the United Nations by US Secretary of State Colin Powell is now widely considered to be a classic example of spin. Powell was attempting to win the UN over to the Bush administration's plan to invade Iraq. These images are part of Powell's presentation.

To the politicians, spin seemed to be a gold mine of opportunity, with proven results. However, the public began to wonder if this were not fool's gold. In the USA, Clinton's critics began to seize upon his reliance on spin as evidence of a manipulative, dishonest nature. In Britain, Blair was accused of being "a control freak", too interested in silencing criticism, a master of presentation but with little substance in terms of delivering policies. Spin was being challenged by counter-spin.

## Is spin dead?

There was clearly an anti-spin backlash taking place around the world. Was this the beginning of the end for spin? After all, Vance Packard's "hidden persuaders" were now out in the open. However, spin seemed likely to survive. Republican George W. Bush, who succeeded Bill Clinton as US president in 2001, had already unleashed a new wave of political manipulation and image building. Despite their derision of Democrat spin, Bush's campaign teams used all the same tricks. Opposition parties in the UK also showed no sign of giving up on spin.

Today's spin doctors are present in almost every government and political party around the world. Sometimes they are outsiders,

At Camp Patriot, Kuwait, a US soldier watches Secretary of State Colin Powell making his presentation to the UN.

professional consultants in politics, advertising, or public relations. Other times they are party officials, or employed special advisers. They may also be campaign managers, press officers, civil servants, or of the official non-party administration.

Spin doctors remain very powerful. Spin will no doubt re-invent itself, allied with the new technical developments of the 21st century, new communications media, and new political priorities. Under various names, and in various guises, political manipulation already has a very long history, and seems likely to continue.

## WHEN SPIN GOES TOO FAR

**DANGER!**

**DO NOT PROCEED BEYOND THIS POINT**

On 11 September 2001 (the day which became known as "9/11"), terrorists hijacked four aircraft in the USA. Two planes destroyed the twin towers of the World Trade Center in New York City. A third crashed into the Pentagon, in Virginia. The fourth came down in a field in Pennsylvania. Almost 3000 people were killed. All over the world, people were shocked and horrified by the images they saw on television.

A spin doctor with the UK's Labour government, Jo Moore, saw the news that day from a different angle. She put out an office email, suggesting that this would be "a good day to bury bad news".

What she was suggesting was that if the government had any news that might damage it, such as an unpopular policy statement or embarrassing statistics, this was the day to tell the press. This was because television networks and newspapers around the world would be carrying one story only: the tragedy in the USA. Any other news would probably not be reported or read, and the government could save its face.

Jo Moore's insensitive email was leaked to the press, and she eventually lost her job because the public strongly disapproved of her suggestion. However, the management of news as suggested by Jo Moore surprised few people. The tactic was already standard practice around the world, from the USA to Australia.

# tricks of the trade

T he arts of political manipulation are sometimes referred to as "smoke and mirrors", a phrase that means "creating an illusion or special effect". Spin, like its related tactics, is no mere trick, however. Politicians argue that presentation is essential for voters to understand certain issues, and they present those issues according to their beliefs and policies. In a democracy, the opposition parties present the other side of each issue, and the public can listen to every argument, and choose between them. Spin is thus backed up by a hard, daily grind, which requires detailed, focused work, and total commitment. It is indeed "a permanent campaign".

*Donald Rumsfeld with a member of the Kuwaiti royal family, who have relied on the PR firm Hill & Knowlton to lobby successive US governments, particularly for assistance following Iraq's invasion of Kuwait in 1990.*

## Rules of spin

If there were a school for spin doctors, the students would be taught three main lessons.

Golden rule number one is that spin is not the same as outright deception. A public relations drive is useless if it is not based on the truth. President Clinton's spin doctors were dismayed when their client lied publicly about having had an affair with a young woman called Monica Lewinsky. A spin doctor's response would generally be to admit the affair but then to deflect the criticism, or to turn it in some way to the client's advantage. This is because politicians lose respect if they do not tell the truth, so spin is about telling at least a part of the truth, but putting a positive and convincing interpretation on it.

Golden rule number two has already been mentioned. The spin doctor must not be seen pulling the strings, otherwise his or her client no longer seems believable. Oncea cunning ploy has been exposed, the client is left looking like a trickster. Even if every word the client says afterwards is the plain truth, he or she is no longer believed.

*President Bill Clinton inspects an Air Force honour guard. It took all the considerable skills of his spin doctors to bring the president through the disastrous Lewinsky affair.*

## Believing in P.R.

"We believe that communication has the power to create change, and that real change occurs only with effective, powerful communication. Communication is the heart of what makes us human, what makes the world go around, and what we at Hill & Knowlton do day in and day out in 70 offices in 37 countries around the globe."

Website statement of the US public relations company Hill & Knowlton, 2004

Golden rule number three is never to lose touch with public opinion. It is very easy for politicians to become cut off from everyday life. They travel around in chauffeur-driven limousines, so they do not know what people are saying as they queue for buses or are packed into an underground railway carriage. They rarely sit in a café, or meet their opponents face to face. They live in isolated political locations such as Washington DC (the USA), Westminster in London (the UK), Canberra (Australia), and the Kremlin in Moscow (Russia).

They are often surrounded by people who flatter them. The problem with this is that if they do not know what ordinary people are thinking and saying, they do not know how popular their policies or proposals will be. They need to know and understand public opinion in order to play to it and manipulate it successfully.

Because of this, spin doctors devised the focus group. This is a small representative section of the public, a collection of people who are called in to talk about their attitudes to various policies or topics.

*The political lifestyle, such as the one in the White House in Washington DC, often leads to leaders losing touch with the attitudes and feelings of the rest of the population.*

Their reactions are recorded and analysed. For instance, during George W. Bush's campaign for the 2000 US presidential election, focus groups were shown footage of Bush making speeches, and were given a reaction button with which to record approval or disapproval.

The focus group may be the next best thing to meeting the public in an everyday situation, but it must be used carefully. A political leader who will not act without the approval of such a group may risk being considered reactive rather than proactive (of following, rather than shaping, public opinion).

## News management

Communications media are the number-one priority for the manager of any political party. An election can be won or lost because of headlines. Good relations must therefore be built up with key newspapers and broadcasters. One way that spin doctors do this is to "feed" exclusive stories or hot news items to their preferred journalists. In return, those journalists' papers do not criticize the spin doctors' party. Another method of getting positive coverage is to try and get supportive journalists appointed to key jobs in the media.

*Focus groups are a vital part of the political process. To be effective it is essential they comprise as wide a range of personalities, cultures, lifestyles, and attitudes as possible.*

# Newspeak

In 1949 the English writer George Orwell (1903–1950) wrote a book called *1984*. In it, he imagined a future world in which the state is all-powerful and all-seeing, and forever at war.

In this world, "power is not a means, it is an end". Historical archives are constantly rewritten, under the slogan, "Who controls the present, controls the past." Party slogans declare: "War is peace"; "Freedom is slavery"; "Ignorance is strength." Truth is twisted. The Ministry of Love is a grim building given over to detention and torture. Language is officially simplified in order to limit independent thought, in a jargon that Orwell named "Newspeak". Words in Newspeak include "thoughtcrime", which means that just thinking something bad about the government is as bad as actually committing an offence, and "doublethink", which means that two opposing points of view are expected to be held at the same time.

Orwell was clearly looking in despair at the regimes of Josef Stalin in the Soviet Union, and Adolf Hitler, the former German dictator, and fearing for the future of the world. Need he have worried? By the real year 1984, the age of Stalin and Hitler had passed, although there were other cruel dictators still at large in the world. However, Orwell might have raised his eyebrows at the ways in which language is used today by governments and the press, even in western democracies. When civilians killed in a war are referred to by government spokespersons as "collateral damage" (meaning that the casualties or destruction were not deliberate), some people may feel they are hearing a modern example of Orwellian Newspeak.

*George Orwell's book 1984 has been filmed twice, in 1956 and 1984. This scene from the 1956 version shows the famous slogan which is most closely associated with the book.*

## The grid

A major weapon in a spin doctor's campaign is a planner or "grid", an ongoing timetable of events and expected news items. This will offer an early warning of potential clashes of news or events which might embarrass the government. For example, it would be a bad idea for a senior politician to open a new chocolate factory or hamburger restaurant on the same day that a health report on children with weight problems is published.

This grid should also highlight those "good days to bury bad news". News released to the press late on a Saturday night, when the Sunday newspapers have already been made up, will not have the same effect that it would on a Monday morning. News may be released during a holiday season, when politicians are not in session, and so are unable to debate the issue. If proposed education reforms are likely to upset or anger teachers, they may be announced on the first day of the school holidays, when it will be hard for the media to find teachers to interview.

If a problem day lies ahead on the grid, the party managers may try to divert attention from it. They may create a rival "news" story as a distraction, or get their president or prime minister to host a reception with controversial celebrities, who

"There are three kinds of lies: lies, damned lies, and statistics."

Benjamin Disraeli (1804–1881), UK Prime Minister, quoted in writer Mark Twain's autobiography, 1924

can be counted on "to steal the limelight".

The grid will also highlight good days to deliver news that will be popular. This may be because nothing major is happening, so the story will get top headlines. It may be that a positive report is about to be published on the same topic as a new policy.

## Leaks to the press

"Leaks" are news items that are released to the press at a time when they are still supposed to be confidential. They may consist of government discussions, planned policies, the findings of a public inquiry, or a private letter of a political nature.

# Fresh leaks embarrass government

## CONDEMNED BY LEADER

In public, politicians generally condemn leaks, because governments are supposed to report important policies or findings directly to elected representatives before they discuss them with journalists. However, it is very often the government itself that leaks information to the press, in a bid to head off trouble before it happens. A military commander would call this "a pre-emptive strike".

There are various reasons for leaking information. It may just be that the government wishes to hand an exclusive story to its favourite newspaper. The aim of the leak may be "to trail" a forthcoming policy on which the government has yet to make up its mind. If this policy receives widespread public approval, the government goes ahead with it. If it is widely criticized, the government can simply say that this unknown leaker had his or her facts wrong, and that they themselves would never even consider such a policy.

Often, a government will leak a very gloomy forecast to the press in advance of an event, privately knowing that the outcome will not be so bad. For example, a leak may suggest that a governing party expects disastrous election results. When the election is over, the results are merely bad. However, the headlines now read, "Election results better than feared", instead of, "A very bad day for the party".

A minister may leak to the press her "private fears" that she may fail to win concessions in treaty negotiations, knowing that she probably will secure a satisfactory deal. The press coverage will then praise her success and skill as a tough negotiator when that deal is finally announced.

## Rapid response

A political campaign team monitors websites, newspapers, broadcasts, and opinion polls. A master of spin has immediate access to a database of well-researched, useful information: facts and figures, the opposition's past speeches, ministers' past voting records, details of ministers' personalities and policies. Political disasters that are waiting to happen must be prepared for well in advance.

*Politicians, such as Australian Prime Minister John Howard, often set up interviews which appear to be spontaneous, in order to condemn leaks, even though they may well have been designed to favour the government.*

When crises do occur, the database provides material for instant rebuttal or attack. Criticisms or accusations must be countered immediately, before they have time to gain currency (become accepted). For this reason, the George W. Bush presidential campaign of 2000 aimed to have a response to any debate finalized within 30 minutes of its conclusion.

In a rebuttal, the facts may be challenged, and so may the competence or consistency of the critic. "You may be calling for higher taxes on petrol now," thunders the speech maker, "but is it not a fact that on 5 May 2004 you said precisely the opposite?"

A radio or television interview is also a potential minefield for a politician. He or she must be fully briefed, and must expect the unexpected when it comes to questions.

The skilled interviewee must get his or her own message across, and avoid the traps which any good interviewer will lay for him or her. To do this without sounding wary, or unnatural, is very difficult. Interviews which are bad-tempered, or full of interruptions or evasions, are not impressive.

**public acceptance 67.4**
**disapproval 18.2%**
**mission accomplished 100%**
**successful 27 829** **un**

**finished**
**likely to proceed 81.5%**

## Facts and figures

Statistics are the backbone of any political or economic debate. Facts and figures are crucial, and they impress the public, too – until the opposition reels off an alternative set of statistics, and a television journalist yet another set. Can it really be true that statistics can be made to mean anything one wants them to?

No, they cannot. However, politicians are often very clever about choosing only those statistics which favour their own case. It is possible for two different sets of figures both to be correct: they just refer to slightly different periods of time, criteria, or circumstances.

Another tactic is "moving the goalposts", in which the rules are changed. For example, a government may be forced to publish statistics revealing that very large numbers of people are out of work. The next month they may announce that from now on, statistics on unemployment will be gathered in "a more effective way". The new method may very well be more efficient, but it may also make it impossible to compare next year's figures with this year's. However accurate the new statistics will be, they may disguise the true picture.

*The public is subjected to a barrage of statistics from politicians. These are usually manipulated to enhance a political message, or to deflect criticism.*

overwhelming majority

condemned by 91%

ir to 328 954

5% sooner

approved by 88.7%

misunderstoood by 28%

## "Selling" politicians to the public

Spin doctors aim to put a positive gloss on failings or unexpected bad news. If a politician makes decisions that are very unpopular, the spin doctor presents him or her as "making tough decisions", "taking a brave stand", "having personal integrity", or "being realistic". Phrases such as "undemocratic" or "out of touch" may be used by the politician's critics, but never by his spin doctor.

Advisers want their political clients to look respectable, active, or attractive. For this reason, clients are often persuaded to conceal any illness or injury from the public, or to present themselves as men or women of action. In the run-up to the 2004 presidential election, John Kerry was filmed performing aqua-sports. Similarly, President George W. Bush had tried to create a movie-style public image when he flew onto a US aircraft carrier to mark the end of the Iraq War in 2003, dressed in a flying jacket. However, many more troops were yet to die in the conflict, and when

*The job of the spin doctor is to make a politician attractive to the public as a whole. Ideally, a politician will be made to look caring and brave, as well as being able to take tough decisions when necessary,*

*On the deck of the aircraft carrier USS Abraham Lincoln, President George W. Bush addresses the nation to claim the military action in Iraq was a "mission accomplished". As the conflict deteriorated, the claim was seen as hollow.*

people later remembered that image, it struck a false note.

The development of "the personality cult" (the treatment of politicians as celebrities, and concentration on their personalities rather than their policies) in western politic has meant that a politician's family and private life are played up to the press. The aim is to give politics a human face, to show that the professional politician is also a regular family figure.

## Put-down politics

Negative campaigning, in which one derides one's opponent rather than putting forward one's own policies, has always been a part of politics. The more one party promotes a personal image of a candidate, the more the other will try to denigrate it. The media can play a major part in this, with newspaper cartoons or satirical television shows targeting a politician's weak spots, and mocking them.

# A PENTAGON OPERATION:
## The case of Private Lynch

It is often said that the Vietnam War, in which the USA fought during the 1960s and 1970s, was lost in the living rooms of America. Television reporting brought the grim realities of warfare into homes for the first time. In the lead-up to the Iraq War of 2003, the Pentagon (the headquarters of the US Department of Defense) decided to ensure that this time it would get more favourable news coverage.

## War reporting

The Pentagon restricted access to war zones except for reporters embedded into military units (that is, they travelled with the units, but had to obey military orders and had to submit to military censorship if it was required). The troops themselves carried video cameras with which to record news. The kind of coverage that US Defense Secretary Donald Rumsfeld wanted was that offered by a television series called *Profiles from the Front Line*, filmed with Pentagon support among US troops serving in Afghanistan in 2001. The two men behind this series were reality television specialist Bertram van Munster and Jerry Bruckheimer, producer of the action war movie *Black Hawk Down*.

## The ambush

In March 2003, just as fears were developing that the US and UK invasion of Iraq might be becoming bogged down in sandstorms and resistance, a propaganda opportunity arose. The US Army's 507th Ordnance Maintenance Company took a wrong turning near Nasiriya, and was ambushed by Iraqi soldiers. Nine US soldiers were killed. A survivor, 19-year-old Jessica Lynch, from Virginia, USA, was taken unconscious to the nearest hospital by the Iraqis, and held for eight days.

## The story

In the early hours of 2 April, the international press was called to Centcom, the central command base for the invasion, at Doha in the neighbouring state of Qatar. Jim Wilkinson, chief representative of the White House, had a moving story to tell. An Iraqi lawyer had bravely notified US troops of Jessica's location. The attractive young woman, who had been slapped and interrogated by her captors, and had suffered from stabbing and bullet wounds, had been liberated when US special forces (Army Rangers and Navy Seals) stormed the hospital under fire. Lynch had been rescued by helicopter, and the whole action had been filmed by US troops with night-vision cameras. An edited version of this footage was released.

The story hit international headlines immediately. The *Washington Post* reported "rumours" that Jessica had fought fiercely before her capture, and had shot several enemy soldiers. There was a rush of patriotic support. Websites were started up to praise the new heroine. There were merchandising and book offers. She was awarded medals for bravery: a Bronze Star (awarded for acts of merit or heroism), and a Purple Heart (awarded to persons wounded in service).

## The sting

Within a month, however, nagging doubts about this story were being expressed in Canada's *Toronto Star* and by the UK's BBC. Doctors at the Iraqi hospital reported that they had nursed Jessica Lynch with great care, giving her their own blood in transfusions. The military hospital to which she was flown in Germany confirmed that she had broken limbs, but had no bullet or stab wounds. An Iraqi doctor, Harith al-Houssona, said that he had even tried to take her by ambulance to a US checkpoint, but had been forced to withdraw under fire from US troops.

It seemed that the Iraqi soldiers guarding the hospital had fled long before the US "assault", and that a US advance party had been informed of this. There was no hostile fire directed at Jessica's liberators, but the troops had nevertheless broken down doors, shouting, "Go! Go! Go!", and fired off their guns.

## A change of tack

Back in the USA, Jessica Lynch herself was puzzled. She knew she had not shot anyone during the ambush; her gun had jammed. She remembered nothing of the events afterwards, in hospital, having been in shock. She wondered if she had been used by the Pentagon for a propaganda stunt, and she was unwilling to play that game.

*Private Jessica Lynch is awarded the Bronze Star medal following her return to the USA.*

The Pentagon was taken aback. It admitted that there was some confusion, but refused to release an unedited version of the film. The Pentagon spin doctors eventually took another tack. They told *Time* magazine that there had been no organized attempt at propaganda, that it was just a series of errors based upon faulty intelligence reports.

## Did it work?

Was this a failure of manipulation? It certainly didn't work out as planned. The UK media officers attached to Centcom were extremely critical of the way in which the project had been handled, and reported their concerns back to their government. However, the Jessica Lynch story did lodge in the US public imagination, and it rallied support for the war at a crucial moment.

# beyond spin

Politics necessarily involves manoeuvring, trying to gain the advantage, and planning strategies. Spin and presentation alone are never enough to win the day. There are a thousand and one other tactics, which vary from the completely legitimate to the dubious, to the seriously criminal.

## Making alliances

Political parties are themselves alliances of individuals and groups with similar ideologies and objectives. However, sometimes the party as a whole must make an alliance with other parties to gain sufficient support to be effective, or to form a government.

Two parties may merge to form a single political unit, or they may form a loose alliance, often known as "a front". A party which forms a government jointly with others is called "a coalition". Such alliances may offer strength through a broadened base of support, but they may also render a party less effective, because it will have to compromise its own plans, and accommodate other people and their plans. An alliance also heightens the risk of argument and division. It is more common for parties to split up into separate groups than to remain united.

## POLITICAL DECEPTION

"It is necessary to disguise this [devious] nature well, and to be a great hypocrite and a liar; and men are so simple-minded and so controlled by their present need that one who deceives will always find another who will allow himself to be deceived."

Niccoló Machiavelli (1469–1527), Italian statesman, in *The Prince*, 1513

# HOW A COALITION IS FORMED

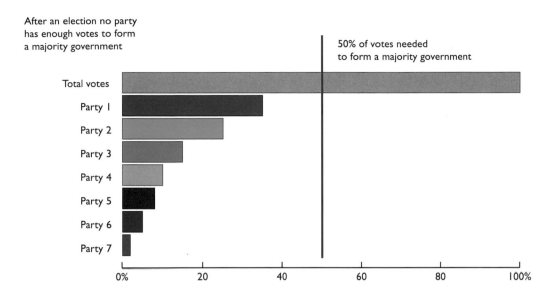

After an election no party has enough votes to form a majority government

50% of votes needed to form a majority government

Following negotiations, Parties 2, 3, 5 and 6 form a coalition which has enough votes to form a majority government

50% of votes needed to form a majority government

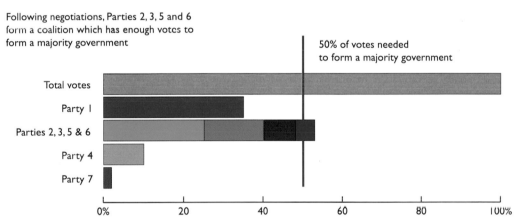

Sometimes two like-minded parties may agree not to stand against one another in an election. They do this to inflict maximum damage on a third party, by allowing one candidate to have all the votes that would otherwise have been split between two candidates. This is called "an electoral pact". A similar strategy is sometimes taken up by individual voters, who choose not to vote for their preferred party, but to vote for the one most likely to damage their enemy. This is "tactical voting".

## Elections and fixes

In countries which claim to be democracies, elections are the keys to power. The rules governing elections are crucial to a fair result. However, they may be bent in many ways. An election in which the results have been fixed is said to be "rigged".

One factor which may affect a poll is the list of people entitled to vote. Are the registrations up to date and accurate? How are votes recorded for people who cannot read or write?

Is everybody allowed to vote? No women, in any country, had the vote before New Zealand changed its laws in 1893. Racist governments may ban people of particular ethnic backgrounds from voting. This happened in South Africa, where before 1993 citizens of African or Asian descent were disenfranchised (excluded from voting in general elections).

The order of candidates' names on the voting slip may affect an election result, as may the design of the ballot paper. People whose names are at the top of a long list have an advantage. There is also a chance of confusion if two candidates have similar names, or if two parties' logos are similar (especially in a society with high illiteracy). The design can confuse people about where to make a mark, and what sort of mark to make. In a referendum, which asks voters a single question about a particular issue, the question's phrasing is important, because some sentences encourage a negative response, and others encourage a positive one.

The technology of voting is also crucial, and became a major issue in the US presidential election of 2000, when the close result was challenged by claims that certain voting cards had not been clearly stamped, and so were not valid.

Many countries are trying out postal and electronic voting systems. Do these offer the same degree of fairness and reliability as a secret ballot in a supervised polling station? Voting by secret ballot was first introduced in Victoria, Australia, in 1856.

*Voters queue up to cast their ballots in India's 2004 general election..*
*The vast Indian population means the voting process is extremely complicated.*

Electoral fraud may involve stealing or "losing" ballot boxes, using rival mobs (or even the police or soldiers) to intimidate voters, or acts of violence. Such tactics have become common in the southern African nation of Zimbabwe, under the rule of President Robert Mugabe.

The voting statistics of a rigged election often tell their own story. In a 1962 election in North Korea, 100 per cent of all eligible voters were said to have chosen the ruling Korean Workers' Party, the only party on the ballot paper. In the 1927 presidential election in Liberia, President Charles King claimed a majority that was over fifteen times bigger than the whole electorate.

*Kim Jong II, leader of North Korea, one of the last hard-line communist nations. It is claimed 100 per cent of all eligible voters chose his Korean Workers' Party whenever elections are held.*

## Money matters

Funding is crucial to success in modern politics. It pays for the canvassers, the leaflets and billboards, the researchers, the spin doctors, the computers, the buses and helicopters, and the advertising. In US presidential campaigns, most candidates come from very wealthy families. Political parties need to raise funds to campaign, and the money may come from rich individuals, companies, or trade unions.

Donors may be people who simply share a political vision and want to make it happen. However, there are dangers in accepting money: donors may be trying to buy political influence with a future government, and all parties have to be on their guard against such occurrences or accusations. For instance, Paul Drayson, the millionaire boss of a pharmaceuticals company called PowderJect, gave a large donation to the UK's Labour Party in 2001. At about the same time, his company won a government contract to supply TB (tuberculosis) vaccines. This caused some people to suggest that PowderJect had unfairly influenced the government, but an inquiry by the National Audit Office ruled out any connection between the donation and the contract.

In many places around the world, however, illegal bribery is a common feature of political manipulation. It may take the form of paying voters for their support, or secretly taking money from special-interest groups or companies. Governments in turn may bribe the officials of a foreign government or a company to secure a lucrative or politically advantageous business deal.

## Cuckoos in the nest

The cuckoo lays its eggs in the nests of other birds, which then raise the chick without realizing that it is an intruder. One political tactic, called "entryism", is rather similar. Members of one political faction or party covertly join another group. Once the incomers are registered as members, and are able to vote on policy, they push the agenda their way.

Sometimes a government will order special agents to infiltrate a political party or organization which the government claims is a threat to state security (or which may simply oppose the government). The agents may act as spies, reporting back on the party's organization or plans. Sometimes they are "agents provocateurs", which means that they urge their fellow members to break the law, so that the government has an excuse to lock away those members. Political parties or companies may also hire agents to break into opponents' offices to steal useful files, or to check their computer databases.

## Truth and lies

The first US president, George Washington (1732–1799), is famously credited with the words, "Father, I cannot tell a lie." Many cynics would claim that few politicians can tell the truth. That is hardly fair, but it cannot be denied that deception, misleading statements, and outright lies have long been used for political manipulation.

One form of political deception or disinformation is "doctoring" images. This was common in the old Soviet Union and its allies in Eastern Europe. For example, when the Czech president Alexander Dubcek (1921–1992) was forced from power in 1969, his image was simply removed from official photographs. It was as if he had ceased to exist.

Today, images can be very easily manipulated by computer. Many photographs in newspapers and magazines have had elements removed or added. Sometimes this is for reasons of design, or taste, and sometimes it is for political effect. When it is politically motivated, propaganda may be involved.

Rewriting history for political reasons is called "revisionism". History plays an important part in shaping politics. Disputes about nationhood, borders, or language are often rooted in historical problems. Every individual and every nation has a different interpretation of history, and it is generally the winner of any conflict who gets to put a spin on the story. However, many conflicts have behind them a version of history that has been twisted beyond recognition.

The control of information is therefore a powerful political tool. Without access to facts, opposition cannot function. A healthy democracy depends on a free and fair flow of accurate information.

A democratic government must allow opponents and critics to express their opinions freely, without censorship. However, states usually reserve the right to limit access to certain areas of information, on the grounds of security. Exactly where the borders of secrecy should lie is always a matter of fierce debate.

## Governor Gerry's map

The boundaries of a constituency may be changed to favour one party more than another. For instance, new boundaries may bring into the area a lot of people who work in an industry that stands to benefit from one party's policies, or a large number of rich people who would support a particular party's tax reforms. These new constituents' votes may outnumber the original constituents' votes, influencing the election result.

Changing the boundaries is called "gerrymandering". The name comes from Governor Elbridge Gerry of Massachusetts, USA, who tried the tactic in 1812. The redrawn constituency borders were said to look like the shape of the animal known as " a salamander", so the new voting district was nicknamed "a gerrymander".

## Political leverage

Political campaigners and trade unions often pressurize governments or other groups to change a particular policy, or to take action on an issue. They may ask people to sign a petition. They may picket government buildings, shops, or factories. They may stage public protests, and demonstrations. They may organize direct action, such as occurs when the environmental group Greenpeace prevents ships from hunting whales.

Workers may strike, refusing to work until their demands are met. Most strikes are aimed at a single company or industry, but a general strike (which calls on all workers to walk out) targets the government. Another form of leverage is called "whistle-blowing". This is when a worker for the government, or for a commercial company, makes the public aware of practices that he or she believes to be dishonest, dangerous, or illegal. This act of "spilling the beans" may force through a change of policy.

Some forms of political leverage are less acceptable to most people, especially in democratic countries. Illegal or violent behaviour may include intimidation, mob rule, kidnapping, torture, even assassination (political murder), or terrorism (a violent attempt to influence policy by creating a climate of public fear). Such tactics may be used by individuals, political groups, or governments.

*Martin Luther King Jr, leader of the Montgomery Improvement Association.*

The word "terrorist" was first used to describe a government (that of revolutionary France after 1789) that ruled through terror. Terrorism by small groups often occurs when people are powerless and have no other mechanism for change.

## Popular action: The bus boycott

One method of political leverage open to members of the public is a boycott. This is a refusal to deal with someone, or to buy particular goods or services, until a political grievance is dealt with.

In December 1955, an African-American called Rosa Parks was ordered to give up her seat to a white man on a bus in Montgomery, Alabama, USA. She refused, and was arrested and fined US$10.

The National Association for the Advancement of Colored People (NAACP) took up Rosa's case, and the Montgomery Improvement Association (MIA) was founded. Its leader was a Baptist pastor called Dr Martin Luther King Jr (1929–1968).

The MIA organized a boycott of city buses. MIA supporters walked to work, cycled, or shared lifts, but refused to travel by bus. Company profits dropped. By November 1956, the boycott had brought results. Discrimination on the buses was ruled illegal by the US Supreme Court.

The impact of terrorism as a force for political manipulation can be immediate. In March 2004, a series of bombings rocked train stations around Madrid, the Spanish capital, shortly before a general election. The Spanish government at first said that it suspected a Basque nationalist terror group, ETA. However, the bombs were then claimed by an Islamist terror group associated with al-Qaeda, the group that was believed to have attacked New York City in 2001. The Spanish public had long been opposed to its government's policy on terrorism and its support for the US-led war in Iraq. When it came to the election, the government was voted out and the new prime minister promised to withdraw Spanish troops from Iraq.

## Campaigns of fear and violence

The chart below is from a report by Amnesty International, an organization that campaigns for human rights. It shows the number of countries around the world where the basic human rights of citizens have been violated or offended by officials. Many of these statistics reflect a form of political manipulation which is criminally violent or unjust, and often condemned as such by the United Nations Declaration of Human Rights (written in 1948 by the UN, which promotes international peace).

## HUMAN RIGHTS STATISTICS

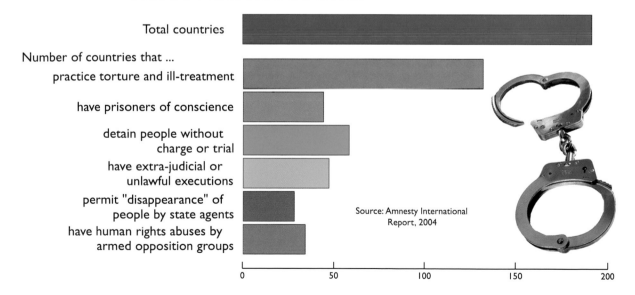

Source: Amnesty International Report, 2004

# the worldwide stage

In the 19th century, Russia, France, and the UK were competing to control Central Asia and Afghanistan. In 1842 a British spy was captured and, before he was executed, he referred to the international manoeuvring and political manipulation of his day as "the great game".

International politics is still rather like a game of poker or chess on a grand scale. However, the stakes are much higher than they are in a mere game. International diplomacy may prevent or cause war, famine, prosperity, or poverty. It may be a matter of life or death for millions of people.

## Diplomacy and war

Diplomats represent a country on the international stage. They serve their own government, and represent its views, rather than their own. Through diplomacy, two nations may build up trading links, help one another, or encourage cultural exchanges. They try to gain political influence and advantage. They try to understand, or sometimes undermine, one another. One country may send agents into the other as spies, to discover its secret plans. When diplomacy fails, the result may be war.

*The world of international politics has often been likened to a huge chess game.*

## The telegram trick

One of the craftiest political manipulators in 19th-century Europe was the Prussian statesman Otto von Bismarck, the man who did more than any other to create a united German empire. In 1870, Bismarck wanted to provoke a war with France over the issue of whether a German prince should be allowed to become the next king of Spain. The French government kept pushing the issue, even after the German candidate for the throne had withdrawn. In reply, King Wilhelm of Prussia sent off a telegram to the French. Bismarck released the wording of this telegram to the press, but edited it so that it sounded much more aggressive than it really was. French public opinion was outraged, and France declared war on Prussia – and was defeated. Bismarck had won the day.

*Otto von Bismarck*

" Politics is the art of the possible "

Otto von Bismark
(1815–1898),
German Chancellor

## Nations and alliances

The political organization of a society depends on the way that its economy functions. In the past there were tribes of hunters, feudal kingdoms based on land ownership, nations based on a monetary economy, and the large overseas empires of the 1800s and early 1900s.

Today nation states (in which people are united by identifying factors such as language, or a common descent) still exist, but increasingly the corporations on which their economies depend are transnational, based in many countries. This economic system contains inequalities of wealth and power, which give rise to political conflict and manipulation on a worldwide scale, whereas previously conflicts tended to be more local.

# Wheeling and dealing at the United Nations

In 2003 the USA, the UK, and Spain wanted the UN Security Council to pass a resolution which had the effect of proposing a war against Iraq. This received some support, but was opposed by many powerful countries, including France, Germany, and China. Others, such as Russia, were shifting their ground.

The USA tried to win over its opponents by using the following tactics.

Promising aid, loan guarantees, and military assistance to supporters.

Making it clear that it would not buy oil for its strategic reserves from countries such as Mexico if they did not offer their support.

Threatening to veto membership of the North Atlantic Treaty Organization (NATO; an alliance of US, Canada, and European countries) to anyone who opposed the motion.

Threatening to use its influence with the International Monetary Fund and the World Bank against the interests of its opponents, and to oppose the award of trading benefits to such countries.

According to press reports in Australia and Europe, it also issued a memorandum ordering surveillance of opponents' telephones and emails to find out their negotiating positions.

When it became clear that France would probably veto the motion, it was dropped. A previous resolution was taken as the justification for going to war.

The move towards a worldwide economy is called "globalization". International relations are, in effect, governed by broad political and economic alliances. Within these, strategies of manipulation similar to those used within national governments, political parties, and public campaigns are used. For example, large-scale versions of the boycott are the imposition of economic sanctions or a blockade (preventing a nation from trading).

A nation, alliance, or economic organization such as the International Monetary Fund (IMF) or the Commonwealth may impose political conditions before offering to help a poor country. For example, it may offer aid only in return for political support, or offer to help build a dam only if one of its own engineering companies is awarded the contract to do the work.

## The United Nations

International alliances help to cement peace. The United Nations, founded in 1945, has 191 member nations, and operates a huge number of agencies working on a global scale for peace, justice, health, and economic collaboration.

The UN is directed by a secretary-general. The Security Council, a privileged inner circle of member states, is made up of the world's most powerful and wealthy nations, alongside representatives of the wider membership, who take turns to be part of it. The membership as a whole sits in the General Assembly. China, France, Russia, the UK, and the USA are permanent members of the Security Council, and can issue a veto, to prevent any policy from going forward.

*The United Nations building in New York, built on land donated by the Rockefeller family. It is home to the General Assembly and the Security Council.*

# what's right? what's wrong? what works?

Political manipulation raises important questions of ethics (moral principles), of what people consider to be right or wrong. What are acceptable methods and degrees of manipulation? Should spin doctors have a professional code of conduct? Who should monitor their activities? Should photos that have been "doctored" carry an acknowledgement that they do not represent the original image? What activities should be declared illegal? How can governments be persuaded that political aims do not justify abuses of human rights?

To what extent the ends justify the means is a key ethical question. To Machiavelli, it was a clear-cut argument. If the result was good for the state, he believed, almost any methods were justifiable. But other people would argue that if the means are unethical, the whole political process is dirtied and invalidated.

IN THIS TEMPLE
AS IN THE HEARTS OF THE PEOPLE
FOR WHOM HE SAVED THE UNION
THE MEMORY OF ABRAHAM LINCOLN
IS ENSHRINED FOREVER

"You can fool all the people some of the time, and some of the people all the time, but you cannot fool all the people all of the time."

Attributed to US president Abraham Lincoln (1809–1865)

## So far, so good

Politics is a mechanism for making our lives better. It cannot be effective without efficient management or persuasive communication. A campaign can rarely be won without lobbying, and it is perfectly reasonable for politicians, campaigners, and business people to be concerned with presentation and public relations. If we have a free press, these people have to work with it in order to get their message across to the public.

It would be a serious mistake to give up on politics and politicians just because they may sometimes be devious and cunning. They perform a crucial role, and their decisions affect everybody's lives. Some people think that deviousness and cunning are basic traits of human nature. It could even be argued that toddlers start learning methods of manipulation when they throw tantrums to get treats from their parents.

## Bad practice and regulation

As the amount of secrecy, deception, or cunning increases, political manipulation enters muddier ethical waters. When does a hint or a suggestion become a lie? When does promotion turn into propaganda? When does persuasion become arm-twisting? How relevant is someone's private

"War is nothing more than the continuation of politics by other means"

Karl von Clausewitz
(1780–1831).
German soldier

life to his or her public career as a politician? These can be extraordinarily difficult questions to answer.

In many parts of the world there are codes, regulations, and laws which guide or control the practices of the public relations and advertising industries, political campaigning, lobbying, elections, and public standards. Regulatory codes are only as effective as their enforcement, and the forces involved are often very powerful. It is hard to challenge a government or a giant media corporation from the outside, and these bodies tend to have little to gain from regulating themselves. To some people, this may explain why spin and other forms of manipulation have proliferated over the past 50 years.

The worst excesses of political manipulation – those that involve intimidation, violence, or even terrorism – may be tackled with national or international policing or intervention. The question is again one of means and ends, however. Are any means acceptable to prevent criminal abuse, or must the means used be ethical, respecting human rights and international law? One has to consider whether any political initiative is possible once the moral high ground has been lost. For instance, should people suspected of terrorism be detained without trial, or is this a breach of their human rights, making the overall situation worse? These are not just questions of ethics, but also of practical considerations, as people seek the most effective response.

## The role of the citizen

Many people blame politicians for the existence of spin, even though they recognize that a lot of individuals spin in their own interests in everyday life. Each citizen living in a democracy needs to identify for him- or herself where the ethical boundaries of manipulation should be drawn. If campaigners or politicians fail to live up to these standards, people can withdraw their support, or vote against certain groups.

*Symbols of political power and political inspiration from around the world.*

The problem with manipulation is not just one of quality, but also of quantity. Some politicians seem so concerned with spin, management, and point-scoring that they are accused of ignoring ideas of substance, genuine policies, and reasoned argument. In this way, over-spinning can be counter-productive, undermining democracy and public debate. This is because people may lose interest in politics, and not bother voting, if they think they are not being offered serious ideas and discussions.

Politicians often accuse young people of apathy or cynicism, because relatively few of them bother to vote. Some young people counter this suggestion by claiming that it is actually the spin doctors' cynical political manipulation which destroys idealism. They argue that honesty, sincerity, and straight-talking could work wonders to reinvigorate political debate and win support for a political party. In the end, it is for the individual to decide on the best way forward – and for society to respond.

# recognizing manipulation

Sometimes it is obvious that manipulation is being attempted. If someone is being threatened or cajoled, it must be for a reason. If a politician kisses a baby on the head just as a television camera pops up, the chances are that he or she is after someone's vote. However, a lot of the time the persuaders do remain "hidden". It is best to be on guard, and to use common sense, to spot the tactics being used.

Not everything we read in a newspaper or hear on the news is the unvarnished truth. It may be a particular interpretation of the truth, or it may be a pack of lies. The first question we must ask is: What is the source of the story? Does the source have a motive for misleading people, or for presenting a story in a particular way?

*Whatever we do, we need to be alert to the possibility of manipulation.*

Who has written or presented the report? Does he or she have an axe to grind (a hidden motive)?

Who owns the medium? Is it a serious newspaper, or a scandal sheet? If the article appears on the Internet, how reliable is the website? Does it have a political bias? If an article is calling for less regulation of the media, is it printed in a newspaper owned by a media corporation that would benefit from such a policy? Who advertises in the paper?

If people are being asked to support a policy, do they understand its implications? For example, they may be asked to vote for emergency laws because of a crisis. Is that crisis really serious, or are the politicians simply trying to curb people's freedom, as happened in Nazi Germany in the 1930s?

When someone is lost in a landscape, he or she needs to take bearings from more than one landmark. It is the same with finding out information. Compare several sources and their content before forming an opinion on a story. Check the facts. If statistics are being compared, make sure that they are comparable.

Consider very carefully the language being used. Is it clear and factual, or emotional and suggestive? Does one statement lead on from another in a logical way?

**assassinate**
murder a prominent person, usually for a political purpose

**bias**
tending to support one side of an argument; not impartial

**boycott**
protest campaign of refusing to deal with someone, or refusing to buy certain goods or services

**brand name**
name used to identify a particular product or its manufacturer

**broadsheet**
newspaper with a large format, generally favoured by people with a more serious approach to news and comment

**canvass**
ask people to vote for a particular party during an election campaign, or ask their opinions

**capitalist**
economic system based on the belief in private ownership and a competitive market

**censor**
limit or prevent free communication, especially if limits are imposed by official bodies or governments

**civil servant**
official who carries out government administration

**coalition**
alliance of two or more parties prepared to stand on the same platform or form a government together

**Cold War**
period of political rivalry between capitalist USA and communist Soviet Union between 1945 and 1991

**communist**
someone who believes that the working class, as the creator of wealth, should own the means of production and govern the state through its own political organization.

**counter-spin**
campaign of spin that is designed to deflect someone else's spin

**database**
useful information which is stored on a computer in such a way as to be easily and quickly accessible

**democracy**
system of government by elected representatives of the public

**denigrate**
put someone down; say bad things about them

**dictatorship**
rule by a single person who has absolute power

**diplomacy**
negotiation between nations or alliances; seeking to influence a political situation by persuasion or political threats rather than by violence

**direct action**
public protest, violent or non-violent, which targets a building or an activity

**discriminate**
treat one group of people differently from other groups

**electoral pact**
agreement between two political parties not to contest the same seat/s during an election

**electorate**
list of people entitled to vote

**focus group**
small representative group chosen to find out social attitudes when drawing up policy

**fool's gold**
worthless metal (iron pyrites) which looks like gold; has come to mean an illusion or false dream

**gerrymander**
alter electoral boundaries to benefit one party more than another

**globalize**
move towards a single, worldwide, capitalist economy

**human rights**
basic requirements of justice, equality, and well being which all people deserve, such as detailed in the United Nations Declaration of Human Rights (1948)

**ideology**
set of coherent political views

**image**
any visual representation, such as a photograph, illustration, or computer display; may also mean the general impression conveyed to the public by a person or product

**instant rebuttal**
immediate response to one's political opponents, countering their arguments

**lobby**
seek support from someone

**negative campaigning**
concentrating on the faults of the opposition rather than on one's own policies

**nationalist**
a person who fervently supports their country, possibly to the detriment of other countries or peoples

**opinion poll**
attempt to find out public opinion on an issue by questioning a sample section of people

**petition**
collect a list of names in support of a public campaign; also refers to the list of signatures

**picket**
stand outside a public building in protest, communicating with those who enter or leave, or preventing them from entering or leaving

**policy**
agreed course of political action

**politics**
mechanisms for bringing about social and economic change; government, or international relations

**press office**
department of a government, political party, company, or organization which deals with the press

**proactive**
taking the initiative, rather than waiting for events to happen

**propaganda**
information, often misleading, put out to support or argue against a particular cause

**public relations**
managing a favourable response to a product, company, person, or policy

**pundit**
someone who sets him- or herself up as an expert or as a commentator, especially in broadcasting (originally an Indian term of respect for a learned man)

**racism**
belief that humanity can be divided into different races and that some of these groups are superior to others

**rapid response**
being prepared for political developments, and ready to react to them

**reactive**
basing one's behaviour on a reaction to events

**refugee**
someone who has to flee from one country to another as a result of oppression

**Renaissance**
revival in learning, culture, and science which reached its height in the late 15th century

**right-wing**
holding conservative political views

**sanction**
punitive measure taken by one country to prevent another from trading or receiving aid

**Soviet Union**
federation of communist states within a single state in an area that included modern Russia. It ended in 1991.

**spad**
slang for "special adviser", a political consultant or "spin doctor"

**spin**
method of political manipulation in which news stories and the media are managed to carry a bias favourable to the person or party doing the spinning

**spin doctor**
press officer, political consultant, or public relations expert who aims to present his or her client in the most favourable way possible by managing news and the media; also called "a spinmeister"

**sponsor**
somebody who initiates or finances a service or action

**tabloid**
small format for newspapers, originally favoured only by the popular press

**telegraph**
any method of sending signals or messages over a long distance, especially electric systems developed in the 19th century

**veto**
Latin word for "I forbid"; procedure for preventing a policy from being acted upon

## Books

Downing, David, **Democracy** (Heinemann Library, 2003

Machiavelli, Niccoló, **The Discourses** (Penguin, 2003)

Machiavelli, Niccoló, **The Prince** (Oxford World Classics, 1998)

Orwell, George, 1984 (Penguin Books, 1989)

Packard, Vance, **The Hidden Persuaders** (Pelican, 1964)

Pitcher, George, **The Death of Spin** (Wiley, 2004)

Tye, Larry, **The Father of Spin: Edward L. Bernays and the Birth of Public Relations** (Owl, 2002)

## Websites

www.pbs.org/newshour/on2/elections.html – an online NewsHour special for students

www.bbc.co.uk/schools/citizenx – website on what it means to be a citizen

# Titles in the *Influence and Persuasion* series include:

Hardback 0431098328

Hardback 0431098336

Hardback 0431098344

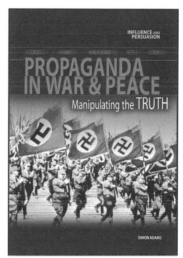

Hardback 0431098360

Hardback 0431098352

Find out about the other titles in this series on our website www.heinemann.co.uk/library